Deer

Christine Webster

www.av2books.com

Step 1
Go to www.av2books.com

Step 2
Enter this unique code

QKIXBVOQC

Step 3
Explore your interactive eBook!

CONTENTS

AV2 is optimized for use on any device

Your interactive eBook comes with...

Contents
Browse a live contents page to easily navigate through resources

Audio
Listen to sections of the book read aloud

Videos
Watch informative video clips

Weblinks
Gain additional information for research

Try This!
Complete activities and hands-on experiments

Key Words
Study vocabulary, and complete a matching word activity

Quizzes
Test your knowledge

Slideshows
View images and captions

... and much, much more!

Contents

Meet the Deer

Deer are **mammals**. They have big eyes and sharp hearing. Deer have a keen sense of smell. They can run very fast, up to 36 miles (58 kilometers) per hour. They are also good swimmers.

Male deer are called bucks. Bucks have **antlers** on their head. Female deer are called does. Most does do not have antlers. In some **species**, such as caribou, both males and females grow antlers.

An adult deer's coat is made up of more than **6 million** individual hairs.

Antlers are made out of bone. Deer shed their old antlers and grow new ones every year.

Where Deer Live

Deer are found in North America, South America, Europe, northern Africa, and Asia. Some deer, such as caribou, travel from place to place with the changing seasons. This is called migration. Deer can move up to 30 miles (48 km) between summer and winter.

Deer species range in size. Some are very small. The Florida Key deer is only 30 inches (76.2 centimeters) high at the shoulder. Other species, such as the moose, are quite large, reaching up to 6.5 feet (2 meters) tall.

The smallest deer is the South American pudu. It is only 10 inches (25 cm) high at the shoulder.

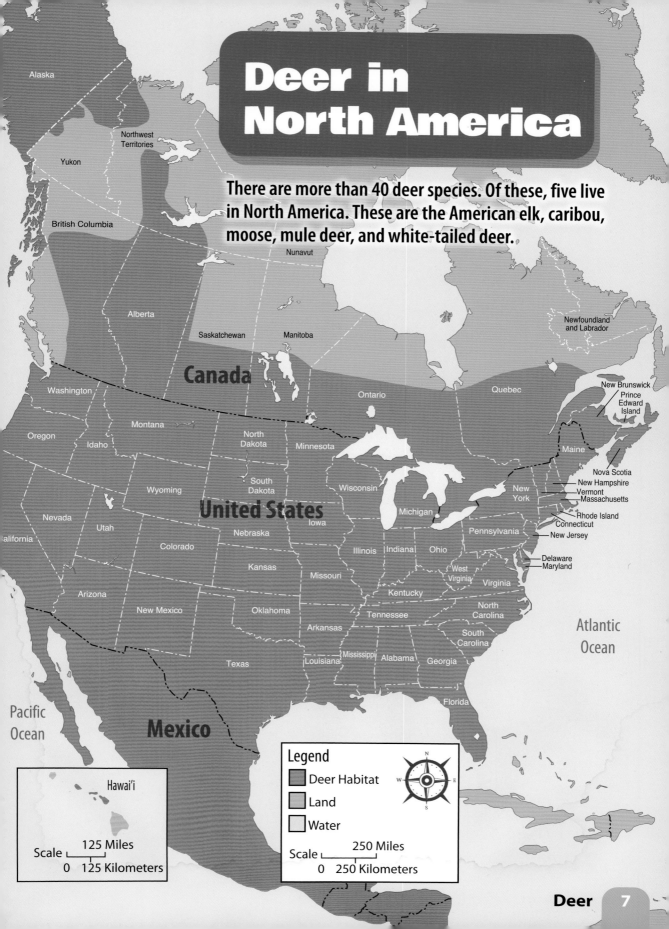

Deer in North America

There are more than 40 deer species. Of these, five live in North America. These are the American elk, caribou, moose, mule deer, and white-tailed deer.

Alaska

Northwest Territories

Yukon

British Columbia

Nunavut

Alberta

Saskatchewan

Manitoba

Newfoundland and Labrador

Canada

Ontario

Quebec

New Brunswick

Prince Edward Island

Washington

Montana

North Dakota

Minnesota

Maine

Oregon

Idaho

Nova Scotia

New Hampshire

Vermont

Massachusetts

South Dakota

Wisconsin

Michigan

New York

Wyoming

United States

Iowa

Rhode Island

Connecticut

New Jersey

Nevada

Utah

Nebraska

Illinois

Indiana

Ohio

Pennsylvania

California

Colorado

Delaware

Maryland

Kansas

Missouri

West Virginia

Virginia

Arizona

New Mexico

Oklahoma

Kentucky

Tennessee

North Carolina

Arkansas

South Carolina

Mississippi

Alabama

Georgia

Atlantic Ocean

Texas

Louisiana

Florida

Pacific Ocean

Mexico

Hawai'i

Scale

125 Miles

0   125 Kilometers

Legend

Deer Habitat

Land

Water

N
W   E
S

Scale

250 Miles

0   250 Kilometers

Deer History

The first deer appeared in Asia about 20 million years ago. Scientists believe that deer once lived only in Arctic areas. They began living in parts of North America about 4 million years ago.

At one time, the deer's biggest threats were **predators**. These included wolves and mountain lions. Humans also hunted deer for food.

Today, humans are some of the deer's main predators. Humans hunt deer for many reasons, including for food and clothing. Despite being hunted, the North American deer population is healthy and stable.

The white-tailed deer is the oldest species of deer still living today. It first reached North America 3.5 million years ago.

The Irish elk, a species of deer no longer living today, stood 7 feet (2.1 m) at the shoulder, making it the largest deer that ever existed.

Deer Shelter

Deer rest on the ground in a place called a deer bed. Deer look for areas that are surrounded by tall grasses, plants, trees, and shrubs. This protects them from harsh weather, such as rain or snow. It also hides them from predators.

A deer bed is about 4 feet (1.2 m) long and 1.5 feet (0.5 m) wide.

Male deer mark their territory by stomping on the ground and making scrape marks in the dirt. They may rub their antlers on trees. This is called a buck rub.

Deer can be found in grasslands, mountains, forests, and wetlands.

Deer Features

Deer have many special **adaptations**. Strong legs allow them to leap 9-foot (2.7-m) fences. Deer can swim 13 miles (21 km) per hour. Male deer grow antlers for defense from predators.

COAT

A deer's coat acts as **camouflage**. It is usually reddish-brown in the summer and grayish in the winter. These colors help the deer blend into its surroundings and hide from predators.

FEET

Each of a deer's four hooves has two toes. Hooves are hard and strong. They give deer **traction** so that they can run safely over different kinds of land.

EARS

Deer hear very well. Their large ears rotate, or turn, acting like **radar**. They pick up sounds quickly.

EYES

Deer have large eyes. There is one eye on each side of their head. This allows them to see in front and behind without turning their head.

NOSE

A deer's sense of smell is much more sensitive than a human's. A deer's nose has membranes that capture scents easily. Membranes are thin layers of skin tissue.

TEETH

Deer teeth are made to chew tough food, such as plants. Deer have **incisors** that allow them to bite. **Molars** help deer grind their food into smaller pieces.

What Do Deer Eat?

Deer are **herbivores**. In the summer, they graze on leaves, grass, alfalfa, wheat, berries, acorns, and herbs. During the winter, deer eat twigs, wildflowers, nuts, and fruits. They will **scavenge** corn, wheat, and soybeans from farmers' fields.

A deer's stomach has four chambers. They help it **digest** food. In the first chamber, acids break down tough plant fibers. Later, the deer coughs up the food, then re-chews and swallows it again. Next, the food passes through the other three chambers.

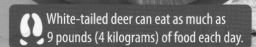
White-tailed deer can eat as much as 9 pounds (4 kilograms) of food each day.

Deer are often fearful of predators. This is why they eat their food quickly.

Deer Life Cycle

The deer's mating season is called a rut. Bucks will fight for their territory during this time. A male will crash his antlers against another male's antlers to fight for a female.

Birth

Shortly after birth, the doe quickly licks the fawn clean. This is so predators do not smell its scent. Fawns take their first step within 20 minutes of being born.

Adults

Female fawns may stay with their mother for two years. Males often leave after a year. At this time, they are considered adults. They are ready to live on their own. Deer can live to be about 20 years old.

A doe carries her young for 5 to 10 months. Does give birth in May or June. Baby deer are called fawns or calves. A doe usually has one or two fawns, but can have as many as three.

1 Week to 5 Months Old

The mother hides the fawn in the grass for one week after birth. This gives the baby time to grow strong. During this time, the fawn nibbles on plants and drinks its mother's milk. At 6 weeks old, fawns stop drinking milk. Their spots fade at about 5 months old.

Encountering Deer

Often, a doe will leave her fawns for hours while she finds food. Most times, she will return. A doe will not come back if humans are nearby. It is best for people to leave without touching the fawn.

If a fawn is injured or ill, call a wildlife officer. The fawn may need to be moved to a safe place. An adult should gently put the animal in a box padded with towels and blankets. The fawn may be scared. It is important not to touch or talk to the fawn. It can have water to drink, but do not give it food. The wildlife officer will know how to help the fawn.

There are **30 million** white-tailed deer in North America today.

People often see deer while hiking through natural areas. Hikers should not feed or touch the animals.

Myths and Legends

People all over the world have myths about deer. Deer are very important to the Huichol people of Mexico. They believe the deer is the symbol of Kayumahli. He is a guide and guardian that only shamans can hear. Shamans are spiritual guides.

The Huichol believed their ancestors came from wolves. The Huichol would hunt deer and offer the animal's blood to the gods or goddesses. This allowed the Huichol to remain human.

In the city of Nara, Japan, people believed deer were messengers of the gods. Today, deer can be found in Nara Deer Park.

How the Deer Got His Antlers

According to Cherokee legend, Deer had no antlers, but he was a fast runner. His friend Rabbit was a great jumper. The animals in the forest wondered who could travel the fastest. Rabbit and Deer agreed to race. The winner would receive a pair of antlers.

Rabbit and Deer were to race through a thicket, turn, and come back. Before they began, Rabbit said, "I do not know this part of the country. I will look through the bushes to see where to run."

Rabbit went into the thicket. He was gone so long that the other animals sent someone to look for him. Rabbit was found gnawing on bushes to clear a path. The messenger told the other animals. Rabbit was accused of cheating. The other animals gave the antlers to Deer. He has worn them ever since.

Quiz

1 What kind of animal is a deer?

2 How old can a deer live to be?

3 How much food can a white-tailed deer eat each day?

4 How many chambers does a deer's stomach have?

5 Which group tells a story about how the deer got its antlers?

6 What is a male deer called?

7 Which deer species is only 30 inches (76.2 cm) high at the shoulder?

8 How long may a female fawn stay with her mother?

Key Words

adaptations: changes that make an animal better suited to different conditions

antlers: bony growths on a deer's head

camouflage: to blend in

digest: to break down in the stomach into substances that can be used by the body

herbivores: animals that eat plants

incisors: front teeth used for cutting and gnawing

mammals: warm-blooded, live-born animals that have a spine, fur or hair, and drink milk from their mother

molars: back teeth that have a broad biting surface

predators: animals that hunt other animals for food

radar: an instrument that bounces radio waves off unseen objects to find out where they are located, how fast they are moving, and in what direction they are traveling

scavenge: to take something usable from discarded material

species: animals or plants that share certain features and can breed together

traction: the ability to hold ground without slipping

Index

Get the best of both worlds.

AV2 bridges the gap between print and digital.

The expandable resources toolbar enables quick access to content including **videos**, **audio**, **activities**, **weblinks**, **slideshows**, **quizzes**, and **key words**.

Animated videos make static images come alive.

Resource icons on each page help readers to further **explore key concepts**.

Published by AV2
350 5th Avenue, 59th Floor
New York, NY 10118
Website: www.av2books.com

Library of Congress Control Number: 2019955088
ISBN 978-1-7911-2087-0 (hardcover)
ISBN 978-1-7911-2088-7 (softcover)
ISBN 978-1-7911-2089-4 (multi-user eBook)
ISBN 978-1-7911-2090-0 (single-user eBook)

Printed in Guangzhou, China
1 2 3 4 5 6 7 8 9 0 24 23 22 21 20

022020
101119

Editor: Katie Gillespie
Designer: Ana María Vidal

Every reasonable effort has been made to trace ownership and to obtain permission to reprint copyright material. The publishers would be pleased to have any errors or omissions brought to their attention so that they may be corrected in subsequent printings.

AV2 acknowledges Getty Images, Alamy, iStock, and Shutterstock as its primary image suppliers for this title.